ANIMALS

Penguins

by Kevin J. Holmes

Content Consultant:
Robin N. Kendall
Specialist, Education Department
Sea World of California

Bridgestone Books
an imprint of Capstone Press

Bridgestone Books are published by Capstone Press
818 North Willow Street, Mankato, Minnesota 56001
http://www.capstone-press.com

Library of Congress Cataloging-in-Publication Data
Holmes, Kevin J.
    Penguins / by Kevin J. Holmes.
        p. cm. -- (Animals)
    Includes bibliographical references (p. 23) and index.
    Summary: An introduction to penguins, covering their physical
characteristics, habits, prey, and relationship to humans.
    ISBN 1-56065-573-9
    1. Penguins--Juvenile literature.   [1. Penguins.]   I. Title.
II. Series: Animals (Mankato, Minn.)
    QL696.S473H635   1998
    598.47--dc21   97-12206
                                                          CIP
                                                           AC

Photo credits
Heather Angel, 14, 18
Innerspace Visions/Doug Perrine, 10; Mike Nolan, 12
International Stock/Ronn Maratea, 6, 20
Root Resources/Mary and Lloyd McCarthy, cover
Lynn M. Stone, 4, 8
Visuals Unlimited/Glenn M. Oliver, 16

Table of Contents

Photo Diagram 4
Fast Facts 5

Penguins 7
What Penguins Look Like 9
Where Penguins Live 11
Penguins and Swimming 13
Eating and Enemies 15
Young Penguins 17
The Emperor Penguin 19
Penguins and People 21

Hands On: Blubber 22
Words to Know 23
Read More 23
Useful Address 24
Internet Sites 24
Index 24

eye

back

flipper

stomach

tail

Fast Facts

Kinds: There are 18 kinds of penguins. All penguins have the same basic body shape and coloring.

Range: All penguins live south of the equator. Most live in Antarctica. The weather there is very cold.

Habitat: Penguins spend most of their lives in the water. Sometimes they gather at spots on the shore. These places are called rookeries.

Food: Penguins depend on the ocean for food. They eat fish, squid, and tiny shrimp called krill.

Mating: Most penguins mate once a year during spring or summer. Emperor penguins mate in winter.

Young: Young penguins eat up to two pounds (914 grams) of food each hour. They eat by taking food from their parents' mouths.

Penguins

Penguins are sea birds. Unlike most birds, they cannot fly. But they are excellent swimmers. Penguins spend most of their lives in the water.

Penguins look awkward on land. Some penguins waddle around quickly. Others walk and sway back and forth. Still others hop from one place to the next.

There are 18 kinds of penguins. All penguins have the same basic body shape and coloring. Each has a black back and a white stomach. But the feathers on their heads come in different colors.

Penguins are built to live in cold water. Their thick feathers and blubber keep them warm. Blubber is a layer of body fat. Some penguins live where the weather is warm. When they get hot, the penguins jump into the water to cool off.

Penguins look awkward on land.

What Penguins Look Like

Penguins have thick, rounded bodies. The feathers on their backs are black or blue-gray. Their stomachs are covered with white feathers. Penguins often remind people of tuxedos. Tuxedos are suits that people wear at special occasions. They are often black suits worn with white shirts.

Penguins are shaped to help them swim quickly. Their legs are low on their bodies. This helps them steer in the water. Instead of wings, penguins have flippers. Their flippers move up and down and push them through the water.

Some kinds of penguins have special features. The chinstrap penguin has a stripe of black feathers under its chin. King and emperor penguins have yellow and orange feathers around their heads and necks. Crested penguins have long orange or yellow feathers growing from their heads.

Penguins remind people of tuxedos.

Where Penguins Live

All penguins live south of the equator. The equator is an imaginary line that divides the earth in half. Most penguins live in Antarctica, where the weather is very cold. Others live where it is warm. Some penguins live on the coasts of South America, South Africa, Australia, and New Zealand.

Penguins depend on the ocean for food. When they are on land, penguins gather together at places called rookeries.

Most rookeries are located on ground that slopes into the water. Here, penguins can get in and out of the water quickly. One rookery can include hundreds, thousands, or even millions of penguins. Living together helps penguins protect themselves and find mates.

During winter in Antarctica, the ocean water near the shore freezes. To find open water, most penguins walk across the ice. Some penguins walk as far as 500 miles (800 kilometers).

A rookery can include thousands of penguins.

Penguins and Swimming

Most sea birds swim near the surface of the water. Penguins dive deeply and swim underwater. They dart around with quick strokes to catch fish.

Sometimes penguins must swim fast to avoid enemies. To do this, they must porpoise. Porpoising means swimming underwater and jumping out every 15 seconds. Porpoising lets penguins breathe without slowing them down. While porpoising, penguins can reach speeds of 20 miles (32 kilometers) per hour.

Coming back to shore can be difficult for penguins. The shoreline may be too steep for the birds to climb. To reach the shore safely, penguins dive deep into the water near the shore. Then they swim toward the surface very quickly. Finally, the penguins shoot out of the water. They sail through the air and land on the shore.

Penguins dive deeply and swim underwater.

Eating and Enemies

Penguins find their food in the ocean. They eat fish, squid, and krill. A squid is a sea animal with a long, soft body. A squid has 10 arms called tentacles. Krill are tiny shrimp.

Emperor penguins dive deep into the ocean for squid. If they do not find squid, emperors eat krill and fish.

Predators eat penguins. Predators are animals that hunt and eat other animals for food. In the water, the leopard seal is the greatest threat to penguins. Killer whales also attack penguins. Swimming is a penguin's only defense against these enemies.

Penguins face different enemies on land. Large sea birds gather around penguin rookeries. The birds are looking for food. Healthy adult penguins can defend themselves. But the sea birds eat sick penguins. They also eat penguin chicks and eggs.

Killer whales sometimes attack penguins.

Young Penguins

Penguins mate once a year during spring or summer. Mating means joining together to produce young. The penguins return to the same area each time they mate. Male penguins reach the area first. They build nests and protect them until the females arrive.

Female penguins lay one or two eggs each year. Both males and females care for the eggs. When the eggs hatch, both adults feed the chicks.

Young penguins eat up to two pounds (914 grams) of food each hour. Adult penguins use their large stomachs to store extra food. They eat at sea and return to shore. Then the young penguins stick their heads into their parents' mouths. The parents regurgitate the food. Regurgitate means to throw up. This is how young penguins get their food.

Newborn penguins have soft, downy feathers. After several weeks, they shed these feathers. Then their adult feathers grow. After a few months, the penguins go into the water for the first time.

Newborn penguins have soft, downy feathers.

The Emperor Penguin

The emperor penguin is the world's largest penguin. It lives in Antarctica. It can weigh up to 90 pounds (40 kilograms).

The emperor penguin can dive deeper than any other penguin. It can swim as deep as 1,755 feet (522 meters) below the water's surface. The emperor can stay underwater for as long as 20 minutes.

Unlike other penguins, the emperor penguin mates during the winter. Only the male emperor penguin cares for the eggs. The eggs require constant attention. The males do not eat until the eggs hatch.

After the eggs hatch, the females return. The females help the male emperor penguins feed the young chicks.

Emperor penguins mate in the winter.

Penguins and People

Penguins have little contact with humans. But humans are a threat to penguins. Many countries send ships into oceans to catch krill and fish. Penguins need this food to survive. If humans take too much krill and fish, penguins suffer.

In South America, fishing boats take billions of fish called anchovies. Humboldt penguins need anchovies for food. Because of the fishing, Humboldt penguins have less to eat. Because of this, there are fewer Humboldt penguins each year.

Pollution also threatens penguins. They can get sick and die from oil and other chemicals. Sometimes people spill these into the ocean. Trash dumped into the ocean can also harm penguins.

Scientists are working hard to understand penguins. The more we know about these sea birds, the more we can help protect them.

Scientists are working to understand penguins.

Hands On: Blubber

Blubber is a layer of body fat that keeps many penguins warm. Try this experiment to see how blubber works.

What You Need

One large bowl of water with lots of ice cubes
One pair of thin plastic gloves
Vegetable shortening
One towel

What to Do

1. Put a plastic glove on your left hand.
2. With your right hand, rub a thick layer of shortening on your gloved left hand.
3. Put the other glove on your right hand.
4. Put both hands into the ice water. Which hand feels warmer? Your left hand should feel warmer. The shortening is like blubber. It helps keep you warm.

Words to Know

equator (i-KWAY-tur)—an imaginary line that divides the earth in half

flippers (FLIP-urz)—body parts that are similar to wings; used for swimming instead of flying

krill (KRIL)—tiny shrimp

porpoising (POR-puhss-ing)—swimming quickly and jumping out of the water every 15 seconds

rookery (RUK-uh-ree)—a place where penguins gather on shore

Read More

Allan, Doug and David Saintsing. *Where Animals Live: The World of Penguins*. Milwaukee: Gareth Stevens Publishing, 1988.

McMillan, Bruce. *Penguins at Home: Gentoos of Antarctica*. Boston: Houghton Mifflin, 1993.

Patent, Dorothy Hinshaw. *Looking at Penguins*. New York: Holiday House, 1993

Wexo, John Bonnett. *Penguins*. Mankato, Minn: Creative Education, 1988.

Useful Address

Sea World
Education Department
1720 South Shores Road
San Diego, CA 92109

Internet Sites

The Penguin Page
http://www.vni.net/~kwelch/penguins/
The Rookery: A Penguin Place
http://www.webcom.com/~jimallen/penguin.html
Virtual Antarctica Science: Penguins
http://www.terraquest.com/va/science/penguins/
   penguins.html

Index

Antarctica, 5, 11, 19
blubber, 7
breeding ground, 17
chinstrap penguin, 9
crested penguin, 9
eggs, 15, 17, 19
emperor penguin, 5, 9, 15, 19
feathers, 9, 17
flippers, 9

Humboldt penguin, 21
killer whale, 15
king penguin, 9
krill, 5, 15, 21
leopard seal, 15
mating, 5, 17, 19
porpoising, 13
rookery, 5, 11
squid, 5, 15